FOREWORD

snowboarding

A genuine, serious sport or just loads of fun? Performance sport or a form of expression for demanding young people? Worth pursuing or a waste of time?

I grew up with this sport; I've come to grips with how it works and I find myself constantly faced with the demands of its athletes. Snowboarding is a very young sport, whose rules are continually in flux and developing. It's not easy to get a snapshot of it or even a general idea. This young sport hasn't managed to integrate itself 100 percent in the mainstream structure of sports. Nevertheless it is characterized by clear values: **individuality, style and expression**.

Snowboarding is both a sport and a lifestyle. It's a youth movement. For me it's less about the seriousness of the sport, and more a new take on values and objectives in sport. The clamor for individuality and its expression has existed for a long time now. Snowboarding has managed to progress fairly quickly to being a mass sport. More and more sports are following it — streetball, newschool skiing, downhill mountain biking, beach volleyball — as new offshoot sports, growing out of classical disciplines. So it's not a waste of time, it's just new.

I find it remarkable that a young sport, which at the beginning of the 90s was dismissed as merely a "youth craze," has already been included in the last few Olympic Games as an Olympic discipline. But it's even more remarkable that the rigid Olympic rules in force are currently being changed to reflect the mood and the stage of development of the sport. It's hard to imagine life without snowboarding. It has developed quickly in many ways and inspires both young and old.

And — in case anyone asks — competitive snowboarding is a performance sport, even though it is so much fun, and all the athletes genuinely believe that each others' victories are well deserved.

Respect!

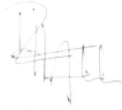

Alexander Rottmann

rider Xaver Hoffmann
location Snowpark, New Zealand
photographer David Selbach

contents

1. BASIC RIDING 8

2. FLAT TRICKS 28

3. STRAIGHT JUMP 42

contents

INTRODUCTION

WELCOME TO THE BOX OF TRICKS!

"How often have I hiked up the half-pipe to practice an FS 540° for the Nth time, wanting to spin really well and land cleanly? The same old mistakes crept in, in fact they were practically automatic and they made it impossible for me to control the rotation. Then finally somebody who was watching gave me a tip: concentrate on a point outside the pipe and focus on it both before and after rotating. That way my head would control the rotation and I wouldn't deviate from the axis. No sooner said than done … and it worked. My 540°s were no longer a problem."

This story shows you don't need to struggle: snowboarding has been around long enough that you don't have to invent it all. Now you can pick up lots of tips and tricks from experienced snowboarders and coaches.

Whether you're just a beginner or a well-seasoned snowboarder, *Snowboarding: Freestyle Tricks, Skills and Techniques* is the manual for you. In this collection of tricks everyone will find something to challenge them. The most up-to-date skills for the half-pipe, rail, kicker and flat tricks are described with the aid of photo sequences and accompanied by technical

explanations. Tips on riding your snowboard as safely as possible are given in a separate section.

This book gives you the opportunity to put every trick under the microscope and remedy sources of error with the help of accompanying suggested solutions. It is designed to encourage you to build up new tricks sensibly and thus to learn them more easily.

Some of the best freestylers, such as Xaver Hoffmann, Jan Michaelis, Christophe Schmidt and Vinzenz Lüps, have personally contributed to the development of this book.

A really good freestyler can cope in every sort of terrain. To get to this level you need a great deal of dedication and perseverance, strong bones and a certain amount of daring. *Snowboarding: Freestyle Tricks, Skills and Techniques* will serve as a reference book along the way.

Have fun shredding!

Nici Pederzolli

photo: alex rottmann

I. Basic Riding

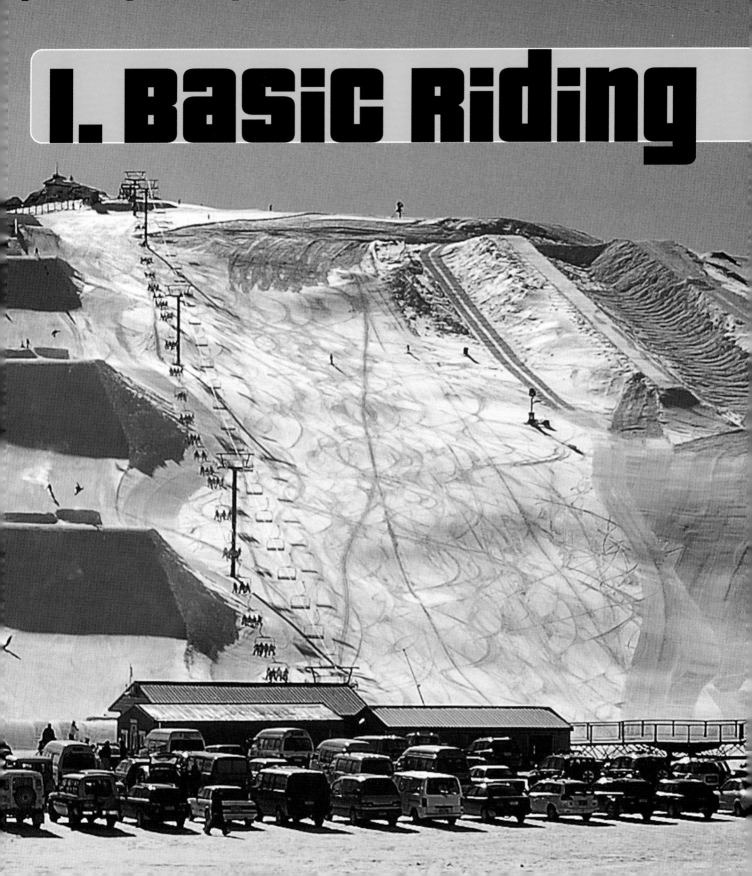

BASIC RIDING

rider _Alex Rottmann_
location _Saas-Fee, Switzerland_
photographer _David Selbach_

STANCE POSITION

In the stance position your shoulders are in line with the board, your head turned at 90° to the board's longitudinal axis.

RIDING STANCE

Your shoulders should be turned slightly in the direction of travel, so that you have a better overall view from the BS while riding, and your legs should be slightly bent. This is important both to absorb impact and to compensate for troughs. Your legs should be like springs, ready to move up or down.

BASIC POSITIONS

To make it easier to describe the tricks, we'll define a couple of positions. For the time being the basic stance position and riding stance will be enough. Later on you'll learn about some other take-off positions.

LOW POSITION

The legs are bent low, but the upper body is upright. The shoulders and arms go down with the movement.

HIGH POSITION

The legs are relatively straight. The upper body is upright, the shoulders go down with the movement.

LOAD POINTS

Even at an early stage, you can practice your stance by putting your weight in different places on your board. This way you'll get to know the flex of your board and get a feel for how much pressure you must use to keep your balance when sliding.

In addition to the classic nose and tail load points, you can also load your board diagonally.

When doing various flat tricks, you need to put pressure onto the edge from the nose or the tail so that you can use the rebound of the board better and achieve faster rotations and more height.

Tail Press

You'll need the Tail Press mainly to do Tail Spins, Tail Slides and Ollies. To do this it's important to bend your back leg slightly and bring your front leg up hard. The basic position should be as neutral as possible.

Basic Riding

NOSE PRESS

You'll need the Nose Press mainly to do Nose Spins, Nose Slides and Nollies. To do this it's important to bend your front leg slightly and bring your back leg up hard. Just imagine that you're trying to slip out of your boots and bindings. Angle your hips slightly, but not too much. Your upper body should not turn at all. You should lean right over the nose of the board.

rider *Alex Rottmann*

trick *Nose Press*

photographer *David Selbach*

BS TAIL PRESS

You'll need the BS Tail Press mainly for FS turns on the piste or on small rollers. Start as you did for the Tail Press and shift all your weight in one movement onto the BS edge. When riding, start this maneuver with a slight BS curve in a low position and then, to rotate, increase the pressure and turn your head to look over your front shoulder.

rider _Alex Rottmann_
trick _BS Tail Press_
photographer _David Selbach_

FS Nose Press

You'll need the FS Nose Press mainly for BS turns over 180° on the piste or on small rollers. Start as you did for the Nose Press, but shift your whole weight in one movement onto the FS edge. When riding, start this maneuver with a slight FS curve and then, to rotate, increase the pressure and turn your head to look over your back shoulder.

FS Tail Press

You'll need the FS Tail Press mainly for BS 180's on the piste or on small rollers. Start as you did for the Tail Press, but shift your whole weight in one movement onto the FS edge. When riding start this maneuver with a slight FS curve in a low position.

Of course you can also just simply shift your weight onto the FS or the BS edge to practice a small rotation on the piste. This works extremely well with, for example, FS 180's from an FS turn. But the disadvantage is that you're completely dependent on your leg power since you can't use the rebound of your board.

SWITCH OR FAKIE

So what exactly is the difference? Aren't they the same? No, they're not. Both are terms for riding backward, but there is a subtle difference between them.

Fakie just means that you're riding backward in your normal riding position. That is, you're riding with the tail forward and your upper body inclined slightly against the direction of travel. The term remains the same for all tricks.

Switch means to ride regular instead of goofy and vice versa. So switch is simply riding forward, but in the "other" direction. The nose becomes the tail and the tail becomes the nose. To avoid confusion, we usually talk about the switch nose — which is the original tail of your board.

NORMAL

rider Alex Rottmann
location Saas-Fee, Switzerland
photographer David Selbach

SWITCH

FAKIE

15

trick _Double Tail Grab Nose Bone_

trick _Indy_

GRabs

trick _BS Air_

trick _J..._

rider Xaver Hoffmann
stance Goofy
photographer David Selbach

trick Chicken Salad

trick Indy Tail Bone

trick _Stale Fish_

trick _Tail Grab Nose Bone_

trick _Kelly Air or BS Crail_

trick _Mute_

trick *Nose Grab Tail Bone*

trick *Method*

trick *Lien*

19

safety !!!

WARMING UP

General warm-ups and warm-ups specially designed for snowboarding are absolutely essential to reduce the risk of injury and increase your co-ordination. Before you begin your freestyle training your body should be up to "running temperature," i.e., you should get your cardiovascular system working harder.

Spend about 15 minutes on a short warm-up without a board. The exercises should consist of one- and two-legged jumps from a standing position, jumping jacks, and rotating and limbering up your joints. Once your muscles are well warmed up you should finish with a few suitable stretches.
Do two or three runs just to get the feel of the ride and to check out the park, then you can really get started.

It also helps to work on difficult movements at the beginning of your training session, while your concentration is still high and you have sufficient strength to nail the tricks safely.

PROTECTIVE CLOTHING

For freestyle you need a helmet and a back protector. They must fit properly so that they don't restrict your freedom of movement. Every fall has the potential to cause some injury, but a heavy fall can also lead to more serious injuries, which could cause you further problems later, so it's very important to protect your head and your spine as much as you possibly can.

If you spend a lot of time riding the rails, then crash pants and knee or shin pads are also advisable.

Trace Helmet

Wrist Guards

Impact Vest

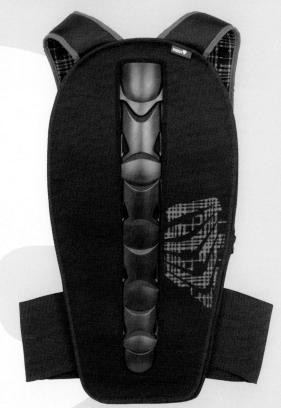

Impact Waistcoat

Rail Guards

Kidney Belt

Basic Riding

Easy Start

rider _Alex Rottmann_

location _Saas-Fee, Switzerland_

photographer _David Selbach_

In the following two sequences you can see exactly what role your head actually plays when rotating. It's important to be able to visualize your trick exactly and know what you should aim for during your air time. Many young snowboarders don't have this ability at first. You'll only be able to describe what you experience during each trick after a lot of practice. But if you remember from the start to fix your eyes on certain points while you're spinning, then you'll never lose control.

I. Rotation – Visual Basics

FS Rotation: For an FS rotation the board turns with the FS edge in the direction of travel.

BS Rotation

For a BS rotation the board turns with the BS edge in the direction of travel. On the rail the trick described works in just the same way. It's only the other way around when doing a Board Slide. A BS Board Slide more or less describes the same movement as sliding on the BS edge.

FS 360°: For an FS 360° your head turns through a full 360°. You can only see where you're going to land at the last minute.

BS 360°: For a BS 360° your head only turns through 180°, since you've already adopted a switch position on take-off.

KEEPING YOUR ROTATION UNDER CONTROL

Head
Your head is your central steering element. By aiming at the specific points you've already chosen, it'll be much easier to control the rotation. With your head you can execute corked and "late" rotations, and you're also in a position to stop them.

Hips
Not only can you turn your hips with your head and execute fast, tight rotations, but you can also stagger the rotations. If you rotate first with your head and then later with your hips, you can also execute smaller rotations, such as 180's and 360's, with great control.

The advantage of this is that you'll see the landing very early on and can better assess just how much you need to rotate from the hips.

Bending from the hips
Bending from the hips serves to slow down or accelerate rotations. Since you have to bend from your hips anyway when executing most grabs, the rotation will be slowed down temporarily. If you let go of your board and straighten up from the hips, this speeds up your rotation — and you can finish rotating your trick.

Feet
You can also change your position and your stance in the air with your feet, independently of your head and your hips. So you must learn to distinguish whether your hand is moving to the board or you're moving the board to your hand.

Grab
Very often the trick you're doing will determine which grab you do. You can't combine every trick with just any grab — if only you could! A lot of grabs would hinder the speed or direction of rotation. See pages 16–19 for some examples of "classic combos."

23

2. Basic Motion Elements

Here are some skills for the piste that you can practice over and over again so that you have an easy time with the basics in the fun park. By working through them in turn you'll see that they're relatively easy. Of course they are, because you've got the time to concentrate on them. If you're sliding for the first time on a rail, or hanging in the air between a kicker and the landing, then you don't have the time to pay attention to details.

For the following exercises it's best to look for a smooth slope which doesn't drop away to the side. Concentrate on the details given and try them all out at your own pace.

rider Alex Rottmann
location Saas-Fee, Switzerland
photographer David Selbach

1...

...10

SHIFTY

non-stop shifties
Really getting the hang of this shifty turn takes a little practice.

shifty vs. Rotation

The next two sequences will help you to move your hips separately a little. When doing some tricks, rotation is unnecessary. On the contrary, just twisting parts of your body in different directions is enough. Of course, this is easiest if you twist your upper body against your lower body. This movement is also called "shifty." It's even easier and also more effective if you twist with your arms as well.

Ride in a straight line and wait until you've picked up enough speed. Now try to do a BS Board Slide on the piste. Keep pushing your front hand in the FS direction. To make sure you stay on track, turn your hips forward so that your FS now faces forward. You're sliding on the BS edge. To reverse this position bring your hand and board back at the same time to their original position.

For an FS Board Slide simply bring your back hand in the direction of the nose and the nose in the direction of the tail. But keep looking in the direction of travel. Your upper body should twist a little. To reverse this position, move your hand backward and the nose forward.

Focus on making your movements appear clean and definite. You'll soon notice that you can really only execute a good shifty 90° turn by turning your hips.

Start riding and keep going straight ahead. Turn from the riding stance into a fakie position, so that your starting position is riding forward and looking backward.

Now begin to turn your hips, but without turning your head. Use your arms to help. Your goal should be to move forward then backward without turning your upper body or your

head. You should be facing uphill the whole time.

Tail Wheelie

Ride straight forward in the riding stance. As soon as you're going fast enough, adopt a low position and shift your weight a little over your front foot. This is the best possible starting position for a Tail Wheelie.

Now quickly straighten your front leg. At the same time, shift your weight sharply backward. As soon as the nose lifts off the ground, pull position you should find the balance to surf for a few yards or meters on the tail.

nose wheelie

Ride straight forward in the stance position. As soon as you're going fast enough, adopt a low position and shift your weight a little onto your back foot. This is the best possible starting position for a Nose Wheelie.

Now quickly straighten your back leg. At the same time shift your weight sharply forward. Try to keep your upper body in the stance position. If it twists too far forward you will bend too much from the hips. Then you won't have good leverage to get the tail off the ground. As soon as the tail lifts off the ground, pull hard again on your back leg. In this position you should find the balance to surf for a few yards or meters on the nose.

27

photo: alex rottmann

2. FLat tRicKs

All the skills that you learn on the piste will make you a better rider. Jibbing is the be-all and end-all of snowboarding. The more secure you are when shredding the piste, the better you'll be on the kicker, on the rail or in the pipe.

The tricks explained here will help you to get a real feel for your board, so concentrate on executing the moves as cleanly as you can. No compromise — style counts.

OLLIE

rider Alex Rottmann
location SaasFee, Switzerland
photographer David Selbach

NOLLIE

technique

the TRICK

You'll need the Nollie as a first step toward rotations over the nose. The Nollie is a very dynamic movement. If you want to jump onto an obstacle with a Nollie you must be much faster than with an Ollie. Since with a Nollie the tail lifts up first, you can't cheat to get over an obstacle. You must already be airborne. With an Ollie, on the other hand, the nose is already moving over the obstacle while the tail's still on the ground.

the Ride

Start off in the riding stance. Before take-off change to a low position and shift your weight onto your back leg.

take-off

From this position, straighten up quickly at an angle forward and up. First push off on your back leg so that your pelvis moves forward. Make sure that your upper body doesn't point too far in the direction of the nose. For best results stay in a neutral position, so that you can build up tension. As soon as the tail lifts up off the ground, pull up your back leg and at the same time push off on your front leg. The rebound of the board will help you to gain height. Pull your arms up.

technique

the TRICK

You'll need the Ollie for almost every surface — from jumping onto a rail, to dropping into the pipe or on the powder, to flying over mountain-top terrain. The Ollie is a very dynamic movement. You have to pay particular attention to timing.

the Ride

Start off in the riding stance. Before take-off, change to a low position and shift your weight onto your front leg.

take-off

From this position straighten up quickly at an angle backward and up. And now watch out! The movement must be well timed. First push off on your front leg so that your pelvis moves back. As soon as the nose lifts up off the ground, pull up your front leg and at the same time push off with your back leg. To get more height you can also pull up with your arms.

Air time

In the air, pull up your back leg as well. In order to bring yourself centrally over the board again, push it under your body: time for a quick grab.

landing

When landing, straighten your legs quickly, ready to absorb the impact.

Air time

In the air, pull up your front leg as well. In order to bring yourself centrally over the board again, push it under your body: time for a quick grab.

landing

When landing, straighten your legs quickly, ready to absorb the impact. You can even roll a little over the tail; this will make the landing even softer.

NOSE ROLL

technique

the TRICK

The Nose roll is a FS 180° turn in which you turn your board over the nose.

9...

tail ROLL

technique

the TRICK

You'll use the Tail Roll to get from riding switch to riding forward again. Ideally, you can also incorporate it to add BS Nose Spins. You just jump from the Tail Roll directly onto the nose and try to keep your balance. You already have enough rotation for the Nose Spin from the Tail Roll.

the Ride

The best way is to ride a switch FS turn. You can also simply add a Tail Roll to a Nose Roll, then you will automatically be in the correct position.

take-off

Lean hard with your upper body in the direction of the switch-nose and push off with your back leg. Now bring your back hand to the front and let the rebound of the board push you up in the air. In most boards the tail is shorter than the nose, but a lot more technology is often built into the tail. That's why rotation is also faster.

air time

In the air you can pull up your legs. Then you can "roll" almost all the way over the tail, but the strong rebound lends itself just perfectly to executing the rest of the turn in the air.

1...

landing

When landing, it all depends on whether you just want to ride farther, in which case you only need to straighten your legs and land, or whether you want to add another trick. If you want to do a couple of easy Nose Spins, then you absolutely have to land on the nose. As soon as you've regained your balance, you should start to lean into the direction of the rotation. And then off you go.

the Ride

The best way is to ride an FS curve in a low position. Shift your weight onto your back leg.

take-off

At the end of the curve, while you're riding on the edge, push off on your back leg and lean onto the nose. With your arms, take the curve you were doing and turn through 180°. This makes the nose your fulcrum.

Air time

While you are turning, pull up your back leg hard. That way you'll move your whole body over the nose, so long as the tail is in front and you can ride fakie. Your back shoulder should push in the direction of the nose as well, and you should let your front shoulder "stand still."

landing

As soon as you've finished turning, land the tail. Load the FS edge again immediately and finish riding the curve fakie.

...1

...7

rider Alex Rottmann
location SaasFee, Switzerland
photographer David Selbach

33

FLAT TRICKS

FS 180°

technique

the TRICK

The FS 180° is basically a very easy turn to do. It's only difficult when it has to look stylish. Then you need enough height to make the rotation seem easy and effortless.

the Ride

Ride straight forward in the riding stance. Just before you take off, move slightly onto the FS edge, from which you can push off quickly later.

take-OFF

Before you ride a curve, jump from the FS edge. At the same time twist your upper body hard toward the BS edge.

Air time

Once in the air you can pull your legs up. That way you won't "roll" all the way over the tail, but the strong rebound will lend itself quite perfectly to executing the rest of the turn in the air. Take your hips and your arms round as you do it. You must realize that you can only land the rotation cleanly if you have enough height. If you only jump up a little way and think that you can still manage it by rotating faster, then you're wrong!

landing

The best way is to land flat on the base and add a simple switch FS curve. That's the easiest way to stop the rotation and your ride will then look steady and controlled.

rider Alex Rottmann
location Saas-Fee, Switzerland
photographer David Selbach

BS 180°
technique

the TRICK

The BS 180° is super easy. It is pretty much made for boring, long, drawn-out routes on which you simply want to fool around.

the Ride

Ride forward as usual in the riding stance. To make the BS 180° look really laid-back, rotate from the tail.

take-off

Move onto the FS edge a little and shift your weight onto the tail. Push off from here. You'll get a good rebound from the tail, so you won't need anything else to achieve height in the jump.

AiR time

Rotation is no problem. You actually only need to twist your hips and land fakie. It doesn't matter if you don't finish rotating in the air. You can also just finish sliding on the ground on the FS edge.

landing

After landing, rotate from fakie into the switch position and keep on riding.

nose spin

rider Alex Rottmann
location Saas Fee, Switzerland
photographer David Selbach

tail spin

technique

the trick

The Tail Spin is a BS rotation. To rotate cleanly, you must first of all build up to it. You'll see that the first rotation is not particularly stylish. You'll only find the balance to execute good Tail Spins when you put more turns together.

the Ride

Ride fakie in the normal riding stance.

take-off

While riding fakie, shift your weight onto the tail and push off with your front leg from the FS edge.

Air time

Your upper body will then rotate in a BS direction. The tail is the fulcrum. Since it's usually shorter and also just a little firmer than the nose, you have to shift your weight backward very hard and also pull your front foot up throughout the rotation.

The next bit is tricky when the nose is facing downhill after 180°. To keep the rotation on an

1...

even keel, you must now push the tail through underneath you and try to get your body to the back of the board.

landing

To stop the rotation, move your weight sharply forward and land the nose on the piste.

technique

the trick

The Nose Spin is a BS rotation.

the Ride

Ride forward in the riding stance and move slightly onto the FS edge.

take-off

Push off with your back leg and shift your weight onto the nose. Then you'll get a BS rotation with your upper body and your arms.

air time

The first 180° spin on the nose is very simple. To spin farther, you have to push your front leg through underneath you and balance more on the nose. As soon as the nose slides through underneath you, the rotation will speed up.

landing

To stop the rotation, land the tail on the piste. To continue riding cleanly, you must also shift your weight backward and make a shallow FS curve

rider Alex Rottmann
location Kaunertaler Gletscher Austria
photographer David Selbach

7...

FS 360°

technique

the trick
For an FS 360° on the piste you need a little more speed, and above all, enough height to control the rotation.

the Ride
Ride straight ahead in the riding stance and move slightly onto the BS edge. Crouch down and shift your weight in the direction of the tail.

take-off
Now Ollie off the tail from the BS edge straight into a rotation. Swing your arms wide in front of you, to make as much of the rotation as you can.

Air time
Doing a 360° all comes down to attitude. You cannot afford to have any worries about edging over. Even if you don't rotate cleanly at the beginning, you can finish the rest of the rotation after landing.

landing
The best way to land after a 360° is to add on a little BS curve to stop the rest of the rotation.

1...

BS 360°

technique

the TRICK

For a BS 360° you should jump off the nose. That way you can again make use of the rebound of the board to achieve more height and rotation.

the Ride

Ride forward in a slight FS curve.

take-OFF

From a low position, push off with your back leg and shift your weight onto the nose. At the same time, pull your back hand in a BS direction, move your pelvis up and bring your head quickly over the BS edge.

Air time

The moment you've built up enough tension in the nose, push off with your front leg and release the nose. Your board will accelerate the rotation through the rebound. Now you must keep your bearings. You've achieved an oblique axis of rotation, by pushing off from the nose. Since you'll rotate faster, you must be all the more careful on landing.

landing

At the beginning you will land more on the BS edge and finish the rotation by sliding. Ideally you should land on the FS edge, so you can quickly ride farther and your run loses none of its style.

...1

...8

rider Alex Rottmann
location Saas Fee, Switzerland
photographer David Selbach

nose slide

technique

the trick

The Nose Slide is very simple. You can feel your way toward it gradually.

the Ride

Ride forward.

take-off

It is easiest if you ride a slight FS curve and push off from the FS edge. You start as for a

Nose Roll and move your back shoulder past your front shoulder.

Air time

As soon as you are balanced on the nose, try to delay your rotation. To do this pull up with your back leg and keep the tail behind you. Then you can glide for some time.

landing

To stop the slide, land the tail and keep riding fakie. You'll stop cleanly if you add a slight FS curve.

rider Alex Rottmann
location Saas-Fee, Switzerland
photographer David Selbach

photo: alex rottmann

3. STRAIGHT JUMP

STRAIGHT JUMP

Welcome to the world of awesome airs and spins. Perhaps you've already heard of Big Bertha, a kicker that was built in Garmisch at the GAP Camp. You have to ride at a minimum speed of 55 mph (90km/h) to survive the air time over an incredible 44 yards (40 m).

Jumping off a kicker is amazing, but it's also dangerous. You can't approach slowly, as though you were on the piste or in the pipe. If you're riding toward a kicker you should already have a very accurate idea of what speed you need to reach on take-off. Otherwise it's far too easy to crash, either on the table or on the flat some way after the landing. But first you should learn the technique for jumping off a kicker.

Avoid sharp curves as you ride. If possible, try to approach it in a straight line from a point that you've chosen. Your eyes should be focused all the time on the take-off.

take off — but how ?

Basically there are three different techniques for getting over a jump. Each of the three take-off variations results in a different flight curve:

Jumping off, Swallowing, Jumping forward

JUMPING FORWARD

This technique is particularly suited to clearing rollers without taking a great deal of air time. Pop an Ollie before you get to the top of the kicker. You'll fly over the actual take-off. Then your flight curve will be flat and you'll land early.

SWALLOWING

If you realize on the kicker that you're going much too fast and you don't have enough time to slow down, the best thing to do is to swallow the take-off. Just crouch down at the take-off point. The fast, low trajectory means you'll achieve a flat curve too.

JUMPING OFF

This is the specific technique for stylish Straight Jumps. Push off with both legs at the take-off to get more height.

With all three variations, it's important to pull your legs up quickly immediately after take-off so you're compact in the air and keep the tension. Your eyes should be focused all the time on the landing slope. Just before landing, straighten your legs, ready to absorb the impact.

SWALLOWi

Before you jump over a kicker, you can practice the techniques on the table. You simply ride past alongside the jump and use the banked snow between the table and the landing as the jump.

TABL

take off

jumping off

jumping forward

rider Alex Rottmann
location SaasFee, Switzerland
photographer David Selbach

STRAIGHT JUMP

STRAIGHT JUMP

1 2 3 4

For Straight Jumps with grabs all you really need to do is bear in mind the basic technique. But try to tackle the grab slowly.

TAKE-OFF

On take-off, jump off exactly as for the basic technique. Push off with both legs, pull your knees up and remain compact.

AIR TIME

Once you're in the air you can start the grab. Always bring your board up to your body and not the other way around, otherwise you'll deviate slightly from the axis and may not land on the board.

If you want to bone or tweak in the air, you can use the same technique as for BS and FS Board Slides on the rail. If you want to bring your leg forward, you must move the oppo-

site hand back. To do a BS Air Grab, pull up your front leg and straighten your back leg. At the same time, you must bring your front hand forward and straighten up in the direction of the BS edge so that you can get into position again before landing. It may help if you imagine your body to be a spring. Twist your upper and lower body in opposite directions, then twist both of them back again into their original position!

Landing

To land, let go of the grab and stop twisting. Straighten your legs so that you can absorb the impact better.

5 6 7 8

9 10 11

rider David Speiser
location Saas-Fee, Switzerland
photographer David Selbach

rider Alex Rottmann
location Saas-Fee, Switzerland
photographer David Selbach

INTRO ROTA- TIONS

As already explained in the chapter on Basic Riding, when rotating it is really important to keep your sense of direction while you're in the air. To practice this, just look for a sloping ramp from which you can start to do small-scale FS and BS turns. The lower end of the half-pipe is really good for this.

STRAIGHT JUMP

When you've got turns in both directions reasonably well under control, you should use the table again. You can practice rotations here too. This way you land on the landing of the kicker, but you only jump from the table. Compared with the half-pipe, the higher speed and the level take-off are an advantage.

rider Alex Rottmann
location Saas-Fee, Switzerland
photographer David Selbach

Now you can venture onto your first kicker. In general, rotations come from jumping slightly off the edge. The more you want to spin, the more rotation you have to get on take-off. But be careful that you don't travel too far across the edge on the kicker and possibly crash next to the landing. There is one particular solution for this.

Ride a couple of curves; do the first one in front

of the kicker from the same edge that you're going to rotate from. So for a BS Spin, ride a BS curve first and vice versa. The second curve comes immediately on the kicker, on the other edge. As a result, you fly straight ahead after the take-off and so can spin perfectly.

BS-ROTATION

FS-ROTATION

BS 180°

technique

the trick

You've probably already noticed from your first attempts that the BS 180° doesn't need as much rotation. Start off by looking for as long as you can over the nose and the shoulder that's opposite to the direction of rotation. This will stop you from turning too far.

1

2

5

6

9

10

BS 180°

take-off

Ride as usual in a slight curve. After take-off look over the nose toward the landing.

Air time

Try to travel "backward" for as long as possible, with your buttocks in front. As you do so, keep your eyes fixed on the landing slope. Your board will be lying crossways in the air, because you've only turned through 90° so far. Just before landing, turn your head away and finish turning the last 90°, so your head shows the direction of the jump.

landing

Just after landing, stay in this position and ride "blind" down the landing. As soon as you feel balanced, change to the switch position so you're looking in the new direction of travel.

rider Vinzenz Lüps
location Snowpark, New Zealand
photographer David Selbach

4

8

FAULTS/SOLUTIONS

You over-rotate the BS 180°:
Perhaps on take-off your head is already turned in the direction of the landing, so you're in a very unstable position because you land switch. If you rotate too far, because you've already finished the rotation on take-off, you hardly have a chance to stop this rotation — you over-rotate. Remember: first the board turns, then the head turns afterwards.

BS 360°

technique

the trick

The fun part of a BS 360° is actually the landing. In this trick, you've already finished the rotation with your head just after take-off, so you've plenty of time for a controlled rotation and grab.

rider *Jan Michaelis*
location *Nordpark, Austria*
photographer *David Selbach*

take-off

Ride as usual in a slight curve. On take-off your upper body is already in the switch position; your head is looking down and controlling the timing of the jump.

Air time

After take-off, look past your back shoulder until you can see the landing. It's not important whether you look along or under your back shoulder. But try not to look over your shoulder, otherwise the table and the landing will disappear from your field of vision and you'll get into a very upright position, which will make it impossible for you to grab your board.

Once you see the landing, keep your eyes on it. Now you have enough time to let your board follow.

landing

On landing, try to put your board down flat. If you have a little rotation left you can go briefly onto the BS then the FS edge to slow down.

FAULTS/SOLUTIONS

You can't see the landing:
You're probably not alert while you're airborne. Before you jump, try to visualize everything you'll see while you're rotating. Try to look for these points again while you're jumping.

take-off

On take-off, make sure your upper body is already in the switch position.

air time

For this rotation do exactly what you did for the BS 360°, but just spin a little faster. As soon as you see the landing after 360°, turn through another 180° and land switch. While you're airborne you can therefore make a mental note of two fixed points. Aim for the landing, turn another 180°, aim for the table.

landing

With experience you're more likely to land after a BS 540° on the FS edge or on the base than on the BS edge. This has an added advantage. After landing you can easily continue riding switch, but if you land BS, you've over-rotated.

FAULTS/SOLUTIONS

You lose your sense of direction in the air: You're probably trying to turn far too fast. Therefore you're looking over your back shoulder and you've no longer got an unrestricted view of everything that is going by underneath you. Approach the whole thing a little bit more calmly. Step by step: look after 360°, rotate farther, land.

technique

the trick

For a BS 540° you only turn your head through 360°, so you land looking at the table.

rider Vinzenz Lüps
location Snowpark, New Zealand
photographer David Selbach

BS 540°

1

2

BS 720°

take-off

On take-off, keep your upper body in a switch position again. The curve you ride to the kicker is now just a little more aggressive. If you glance under your back shoulder when you jump, then you'll turn slightly.

technique

the trick

The more you can spin, the simpler the rotations will be when they're a little corked. For a BS 720°, you turn through 540° with your head, so you land looking downhill.

air time

If your turn is a little corked, you'll see the table first. After about 360° you'll lose sight of the ground. Look at your board until you see the ground again. At that moment you must try to pull the nose through beneath your body and straighten up your upper body, turning your head farther in the direction of the tail and pulling your back elbow up hard.

7

rider Flo Mausser
location Cardrona, New Zealand
photographer David Selbach

8

9

Landing

The landing for a BS 720° is sketchy, since you will land mostly on the BS edge. But it would also be correct to land on the base or almost on the FS edge. Only when you succeed in doing that will you have finished rotating the BS 720°.

FAULTS/SOLUTIONS

You lose your sense of direction in the air. Have you really thought about your visual aids or your fixed points? Perhaps you've released the tension in your body while spinning. This often happens when you simply lose sight of the ground. Without tension in your body, you also lose rotation. You turn much more slowly and will never finish the 720°. As a result, you land on your buttocks and the BS edge.

Therefore concentrate specifically on keeping the tension and turning quickly. When doing grabs, pull the board up harder and turn your head even farther toward the tail. You'll see that you'll soon get the hang of it.

straight jump

technique

the trick

You can, of course, also jump off switch for a BS spin. The movements hardly change at all. For example, here is an illustration of a switch BS 540°.

1

2

3

6

7

8

SW BS 540°

rider Vinzenz Lüps
location Snowpark, New Zealand
photographer David Selbach

58

STRAIGHT JUMP

FS 180°

rider Jan Michaelis
location Nordpark, Austria
photographer David Selbach

technique

the trick

The FS 180° is a little sketchy to land. The turn itself is very easy.

landing

On landing, turn your board and your hips farther. Your upper body turns after take-off, but only very little. Straighten your legs to absorb the landing.

Air time

When you're in the air, you must try to hold back a little on the rotation. Your upper body has already turned through 90°, so follow it with your hips and the board. As soon as you're compact in the air, do a grab.

FAULTS/SOLUTIONS

You turn too far and land hard on the FS edge:
As already mentioned, your upper body hardly turns any more after take-off. You land straight in the switch position. Try to turn just your hips. Throughout the trick, you should be looking at the landing.

take-off

On take-off, your upper body is already turned a lot. Your chest faces downhill.

5

4

3

10

9

8

FS 360°

14

13

technique

the trick

With an FS 360° you see the landing just before you make contact with the snow. That way, your head also turns through 360°.

take-off

On take-off, your upper body is already turned so your chest faces downhill. Your head is inclined over your back shoulder. Look toward the take-off and focus on it.

air time

Keep turning while you're in the air. Try to keep your eyes on the take-off, the table and finally the landing while you're turning — it's the only way to keep a sense of direction.

landing

Generally you land on the base, but a little on the BS edge. You can easily turn a little too far so you can't immediately control the rest of the rotation on landing. This tells you that you can afford to turn more

2

1

7

6

12

11

Xaver Hoffmann
Snowpark, New Zealand
David Selbach

FAULTS/SOLUTIONS

You over-rotate and have to turn even more to ride switch on landing:

This could possibly be the result of trying too hard to get an early look at the landing. But it means that you also finish turning too early.

Start again on a small, lateral edge on or off piste, and remember as much as possible of what you see while you're turning.

slowly. As already indicated, you only see the landing just before you make contact with the snow.

technique

the trick

The FS 540° basically works the same way as the FS 360°.

FS 540°

4

5

take-off

On take-off, your upper body has already turned so your chest faces downhill. Your head is inclined over your back shoulder. Look toward the take-off and focus on it.

8

air time

Keep turning while you're in the air. Try to register the take-off, the table and finally the landing while you're turning, to keep a sense of direction. When you see the landing, keep your head and your upper body in this position. Just turn your hips and the board through a farther 180° and land switch.

9

12

13

14

2

3

7

rider *Vinzemz Lueps*
location *Snowpark, New Zealand*
fotographer *David Selbach*

Landing

Generally you land on the base, but a little on the FS edge. Landing an FS 540° probably won't cause you any problems if you have rotated accurately.

11

16

FAULTS/SOLUTIONS

You land, having rotated too far:
The board actually lands correctly, but your upper body is facing too far over in the direction of the BS edge.

If you haven't rotated far enough for an FS 540°, you have to start the last 180° through a counter-rotation in your upper body. To avoid this, you must get more rotation on take-off.

STRAIGHT JUMP

technique

the trick

There is a substantial difference between an FS 540° and an FS 720°. For a FS 540°, your head must only rotate part of the way, i.e., through 360°, while for an FS 720° it rotates through the full 720°.

take-off

On take-off, your upper body is already turned so your chest faces downhill. Your head is inclined over your back shoulder. Look toward the take-off and focus on it.

air time

Keep turning while you're in the air. Mentally count the turns and concentrate on spotting the landing a second time as fast as you can. That way you will not lose your sense of direction.

rider Flo Mausser
location Cardrona, New Zealand
photographer David Selbach

FS 720°

Landing

Generally you land on the base. FS 720°s are tough to land too.

FAULTS/SOLUTIONS

You don't rotate cleanly and keep going crooked in the air. In addition you lose the tension in your body:

You're probably trying to rotate too fast with your head and forgetting that you should incline it to the side on take-off, so that you rotate better corked. If you look over your shoulder, you'll automatically bend over backward while you're rotating. Not only will you lose tension by doing that, but it will also be very difficult to do a grab.

67

STRAIGHT JUMP

SW FS 180°

rider Jan Michaelis
location Nordpark, Austria
photographer David Selbach

68

technique

the trick

You can, of course, also jump off switch for an FS spin. The movement hardly changes at all. For example, here is an illustration of an FS 180°.

photo: alex rottmann · pipeshape: nordpark/seegrube, Austria

4. HaLF-PiPE

I. Ride the Pipe

the trick

If you're riding the half-pipe for the first time, you need to know that you can't do jumps in it. Imagine the half-pipe as a piste that is built up on both sides so it's in a U-shape. So long as you don't go over the coping with your board, you will "ride" a curve within the pipe. Your board won't lose contact with the ground until you've enough speed to ride out of the pipe.

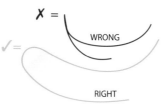

$X =$ WRONG

$\checkmark =$ RIGHT

In order to master "riding" smoothly, you have to bear in mind the following things:

Ride slowly over the flat and remain in a low position. Try to ride on the edge in the transition as little as possible. And straighten your legs as well. Now ride up the wall in this position. As soon as you slow down you'll ride a curve. Bear in mind that you don't go onto

rider Alex Rottmann
location SaasFee, Switzerland
photographer David Selbach

the edge until the end of the curve. You will ride to the end of the curve on the "outside edge."

Once you're dropping down the transition, bend your legs again. Keep still as you cross the flat to the tranny on the other side.

You'll quickly pick up speed using this technique. After traversing the pipe a few times you'll eventually reach the coping. At this point it's important not to lose your rhythm. Straighten your legs early on in the tranny and ride up the wall. If you have enough speed you'll "ride" out of the pipe — keep still. Your

board should leave the pipe as though it's on rails. Once the tail is in the air pull up your legs and get ready for the landing. If you've got everything right so far, you'll land perfectly with legs bent on the edge of the wall on the vert of the pipe.

HALF-PIPE
2. Ride the Air-to-Fakie

rider *Alex Rottmann*
location *SaasFee, Switzerland*
photographer *David Selbach*

the trick

Basically the same principle applies for all the hits in the pipe. You shouldn't jump just for height, but also for distance. Your body describes a curve in flight every time, including the Alley-Oops.

A lot of people make the mistake of riding on the edge at a sharp angle out of the pipe and landing again in the same place.

When you ride out of the pipe at a sharp angle, you certainly get the height, but you don't get the distance. You more or less stop at the highest point of your Alley-Oops and then fall back down again. And you can't position your board so that you can land perfectly. Remember: a body in motion is always more stable than a body at rest.

When you're practicing this, remember: first you ride, then you fly. Ride up the wall. At the highest point look down into the pipe and turn your board across the direction of travel. Here, too, you should try to travel backward

the TRICK

Basically the same principle applies for all the hits in the pipe. You shouldn't jump just for height, but also for distance. Your body describes a curve in flight every time, including the Air-to-Fakie.

A lot of people make the mistake of riding on the edge at a sharp angle out of the pipe and landing again in the same place.

When you ride out of the pipe at a sharp angle, you certainly get the height, but you don't get the distance. You more or less stop at the highest point of your Air-to-Fakie and then fall back down again. And you can't position your board so that you can land perfectly. Make a note of the following: a body in motion is always more stable than a body at rest.

When you're practicing this, remember: first you ride, then you fly. Ride up the wall and at the highest point try to travel backward in the direction of the BS edge. Focus on the coping from the beginning. Even when you're dropping down, keep looking at the same spot. Only when you get to the flat do you turn around and focus on the new wall, where you now have to deal with switch.

while you're rotating. At the beginning your arms can be a real help. It's important that you get onto the uphill edge again while still in the wall.

3. Ride some alley-oops

HALF-PIPE

DROP IN FS + BS

technique

the trick

It's easiest to begin the Drop In at the very top or the very bottom. The walls are not so high or steep.

the Ride

Ride parallel to the coping at a low speed. When you aim for your Drop In point, go slightly onto the edge, but only enough to guide your board. The angle at which you drop in should be very flat — as if you were going to ride a long, drawn-out curve.

Drop In

As soon as the nose reaches the lip, shift your weight sharply — onto your front leg and at the same time into the pipe. Both legs sink down, the hips sink down, and the rib cage will rest on the knees. With a BS Drop In it will feel as though you want to quickly sit down on a chair. With an FS Drop In imagine that you're falling dramatically to your knees. When you drop in you shouldn't lose contact with the ground.

In the pipe ride on the uphill, edge in the direction of the opposite tranny.

VARiATiONS:

- Drop In with Ollie

rider Xaver Hoffmann
location Cardrona, New Zealand
photographer David Selbach

take 1

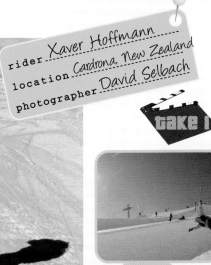

FAULTS/SOLUTiONS

No contact with the ground after the Drop In — flat landings:

- Too sharp an angle as you ride in
- No sitting-down or falling-to-your-knees movement

Too high a speed at the beginning of the "landing" on the downhill edge:

- No sitting-down or falling-to-your-knees movement

77

OLLIE tO BS AND FS DROP IN

rider Xaver Hoffmann
location Cardrona, New Zealand
photographer David Selbach

technique

the TRICK

When you can control a normal Drop In and need more speed, you should move on to Ollie to Drop In.

the RiDe

Ride as if you were going to jump in a curve. Land the Ollie Nose-Dive style. It is also important to get quickly into a forward lean position in the air so that you land on the steep wall of the pipe. After you've jumped the Drop In, you can easily turn your board and your torso 80° toward the coping and land hard on the uphill edge. That way you can steer straight to the opposite wall — that's the right way to gain momentum.

FAULTS/SOLUTIONS

No contact with the ground after the Drop In — flat landings:
• Ollie popped too steeply
• No sitting-down or falling-to-your-knees movement
• Too high a speed to begin with

Landing on the downhill edge:
• No sitting-down or falling-to-your-knees movement

VARiations:

• Ollie to BS 180° Switch Drop In
• Ollie to FS 180° Switch Drop In

HALF-PIPE

technique

the trick

With the basic half-pipe technique you can already manage to ride out over the coping. Now you need to get as much air time as possible.

Basically you can say that the faster you go, the higher you go! But speed is not everything. You also need the correct technique to jump the high airs in a controlled way and to land safely.

take-off

You have to imagine that your board is riding off the wall as though on rails. The biggest mistake is to release the board too early from the wall. On take-off you should neither sink to your knees nor straighten your legs. Just concentrate entirely on riding off the wall. Shift your weight just slightly onto your back leg and load the tail. Even if the nose is right over the lip, you can still keep the tail on track for a moment in order to launch out of the pipe — just as though you're on rails.

air time

In the air, grab your board. Let it slide into your hand as you bend your legs. That way you'll keep more tension in your upper body and be more stable. During airs, look at the coping to control the height and distance of your flying phase. For Straight Airs rotate through about 100°. This happens quite automatically. But you still need to control the air. Use your free hand to control your rotation. You can use it to speed up or slow down your rotation.

rider *Xaver Hoffmann*
location *Mt. Hood, USA*
photographer *David Selbach*

1. FS AIRS

Landing

Just before you land, take your hand off the board and check once more how far your upper body is from the wall. Ideally you should land high up on the vert or on the upper part of the transition. To do this you can straighten or bend your legs to adjust the landing.

FAULTS/SOLUTIONS

You land on the flat:
Of course we're presuming that the pipe's the right shape!
On take-off, push off from the wall. Try to straighten your legs earlier and just ride out of the pipe on take-off.

straight airs

rider Jan Michaelis
location Lake Placid, USA
photographer David Selbach

2. BS AiRS

rider Christophe Schmidt
location Nordpark, Austria
photographer David Selbach

STRAIGHT AIRS

P. 77

85

rider Vinzenz Lüps
location Nordpark, Austria
photographer David Selbach

rider **Xaver Hoffmann**
location **Valle Nevado, Chile**
photographer **David Selbach**

BS ALLEY-OOP

technique

the trick

For an Alley-Oop you lean very slightly to jump from the edge. But the flatter you ride up the wall, the better your Alley-Oop will be.

take-off

You start as for an Air-to-Fakie. Ride off on the tail, focus on the take-off point, bend your upper body and let your pelvis pull forward slightly.

Air time

You can control the whole rotation with your head. As soon as you leave the take-off point and start looking across the direction of flight into the pipe, begin to turn your whole body in the Alley-Oop. At the same time make a Stale Fish Grab — that way your shoulders will already be in position in good time for landing. With a small rotation of the hips you can speed up, slow down or even delay the rotation. Your front hand can help with this, but it looks more stylish if your front hand stays still and straight in the air.

rider Xaver Hoffmann
location Mt. Hood, USA
photographer David Selbach

STALE FISH

Landing
Just before landing, try to bring your knees a little farther forward. It helps to land slightly on the BS edge. You can control your upper body position a little more with your front hand.

FAULTS/SOLUTIONS
No traveling:
• You jumped too hard off the edge
Flat landing:
• You jumped too hard off the edge
• Rotation introduced while jumping

VARIATIONS:
• Tail Grab
• Mute Grab
• Japan Air

half-pipe

technique

the trick

The strange thing about an FS Alley-Oop is that you just don't see your landing. But if you do see it, you've rotated too far.

take-off

Ride in a neutral position high up the wall. Focus on the coping behind your BS edge.

air time

You can control the whole rotation with your head. As soon as you leave the take-off point and start looking across the direction of flight to the coping, begin to turn your whole body in the Alley-Oop. At the same time make a grab. Try to keep your hips across the rotation for a while, as if you were twisting your upper body across your lower body like a corkscrew.

landing

Wait until the last possible moment before you turn your hips into the correct position for landing. Keep looking at the coping, and out of the corner of your eye you'll see how far you still are from the landing. Land on the FS edge. Don't look at the new wall until after you've landed.

FS ALLEY-OOP, INDY

take 2

FAULTS/SOLUTIONS
No traveling:
• You jumped too hard off the edge
Flat landing:
• You jumped too hard off the edge

VARIATIONS:
• Lien
• Stale Fish
• Tail

rider Tobi Strauss
location Cardrona, New Zealand
photographer David Selbach

AiR-to-FAKie, LieN

technique

the trick

Generally you should have a similar flight curve for Air-to-Fakies as you have for normal airs. The biggest, most frequent mistake, is to jump too steeply and off the edge.

take-off

You should simply push off when the tail is still in contact with the snow. Try to aim for the take-off point and keep your eyes on it. Now let your pelvis pull backward a little and adopt a slightly crouched position. Don't worry about traveling backward — that's correct.

Air time

As soon as you are airborne you can start to make a grab. Try to push your hand and your front leg forward while you are doing the Lien. The more bent over your upper body is, the more easily you'll achieve this. Don't take your eyes off the take-off point or the coping below you.

FAULTS/SOLUTIONS

Landing not clean:
- Your head turns too early in the direction of the new tranny
- Your upper body rotates while you're airborne

No traveling:
- Take-off is too hard off the edge
- You're worrying about traveling backward
- Your pelvis only moves upward

VARIATIONS:
- Tail Grab
- Double Tail Grab
- BS Grab

rider **Xaver Hoffmann**
location **Mt. Hood, USA**
photographer **David Selbach**

Landing
This is the trickiest part. To land cleanly you should keep your eyes on the take-off point. Don't look at the new tranny. Don't turn your head and get ready for the next wall until you have full contact with the snow.

rider Xaver Hoffmann
location Nordpark, Austria
photographer David Selbach

NOKIA NOKIA

VALLE NEVADO
VALLE NEVADO
CHILE
www.vallenevado.com

VALLE NEVADO

rider Xaver Hoffmann
location Valle Nevado, Chile
photographer David Selbach

95

HALF-PIPE

rider Xaver Hoffmann
location Snowpark, New Zealand
photographer David Selbach

hand Plant

rider Tobi Strauss
location Snowpark, New Zealand
photographer David Selbach

rider Phips Strauss
location Cardrona, New Zealand
photographer David Selbach

technique

the trick
For a Hand Plant you need far less speed than for an air. You can incorporate it perfectly in the last hit.

take-off
You can ride really steeply up the wall. Coming out from the transition, press against the edge as if you were going to ride a tight curve. This way the upper body is twisted sharply.

air time
As soon as you can see over the coping, press against the lip with your back hand. Push off from the edge as hard as you can with your legs. At the same time pull your pelvis up. Guide your board with your hand while you're doing this. When you

feel that you're vertical you can bend your upper body back really hard once more as for a BS Air.

landing
Now your movements need to follow each other very quickly. The most important thing is to get your board underneath your body again. As soon as you let go of the Hand Plant, pull up your legs. You can briefly push off a little from the lip with your supporting hand to bring your upper body into a more upright position. Ride switch in the pipe.

rider Xaver Hoffmann
location Northstar, USA
photographer David Selbach

Rotations

BS 360°

technique

the trick

For a BS 360° you don't need too much rotation. Since it is easy to rotate, it's often preferred to the switch Drop In, when you're practicing switch tricks.

take-off

Aim for a short take-off, rotate your torso and your head in the direction of the tail, and look at the coping beneath your legs. The elbows are taken upward behind your body. This movement is quite enough to start the rotation. And you'll automatically bring your upper body into the correct position.

air time

As soon as you leave the pipe, pull up your legs and grab your board. Look along the coping and stop the rotation, while you aim for the landing point on the deck. An even better way to stop the rotation is to lift your arms up just before landing. Of course, it looks better if you stay compact when you do the grab, and land easy.

rider Jan Michaelis
location Mt. Hood, USA
photographer David Selbach

Landing

Be careful to land on the correct edge.

FAULTS/SOLUTIONS

Over-rotating:

- You look at the new transition too early
- Your arms don't stop the rotation

- On take-off your head doesn't point downward to the coping, but rotates too quickly in the direction of the landing.

Landing on the downhill edge:

- This often happens with too little air time. The upper body and arms have to summon up too much rotation. This throws you slightly off your axis of rotation.

VARIATIONS:

Lien or Stale Fish. It'll be more difficult with the nose or tail, since you've hardly any time to execute the movement slowly enough.

half-pipe
technique
the trick

The feel of the movement of a BS 5 is nothing like that of a BS 3. Your head and upper body have to rotate for longer. The axis of rotation is basically more on the diagonal. The BS 540° is best when rotated inverted.

take-off

Start off by aiming briefly for the take-off. Now rotate your head and torso in the direction of the tail, inclining your torso a little at the same time.

On take-off, your buttocks form the highest point. The back arm swings while the torso rotates.

air time

Now pull your back elbow up as quickly as possible in the direction of the sky. This brings you into the correct position and gives you enough rotation. Now grab the board. Focus briefly on the coping, and then try to look over your shoulder. If you want to rotate really well,

BS 540°

BS 540°

you have to turn your hips hard in the direction of the landing. To do this, simply push your back knee in the direction of the tail.

Landing

Shortly before landing, push your front leg forward. Your upper body comes over the board, and you land FS. You should be looking in the direction of the new tranny.

FAULTS/SOLUTIONS

Too little rotation:
• Not twisting enough on take-off
• Elbows not pushed up far enough
• Focusing on the coping

Landing on the BS edge:
• Too little rotation
• Not looking over your shoulder
• Back arm doesn't keep pulling right to the end

rider Jan Michaelis
location Mt. Hood, USA
photographer David Selbach

technique

the trick

The Rodeo is a relatively easy 540° turn, but the landing is a bit sketchy. You can easily press too hard on the edge and land in the flat after the trick. To avoid this, concentrate on riding up the wall as flat as possible so that you also travel a little in the air. If you ride the wall too hard on the edge, you'll squash up and catapult backward onto the flat like a spring.

take-off

On take-off, pull up hard with your front leg. Your head looks between your legs into the pipe. Try to remain very compact on take-off.

air time

In the air, quickly try to find your take-off point again. As you're rotating through 360°, first you see the wall, then the coping and later your take-off point. As soon as you see it, rotate your hips through the last 180° so that you can land forward again.

ALLEY-OOP RODEO

rider *Phips Strauss*
location *Cardrona, New Zealand*
photographer *David Selbach*

landing

On landing, bend your legs and land on the uphill edge.

FAULTS/SOLUTIONS

You keep landing on the flat:
As already mentioned, it's important not to not to ride too steeply up the wall. And under no circumstances straighten your legs on the vert — just pull up on your front leg.

If you find it difficult to visualize the movement, then remember how you stood up when you were a beginner. Just lie down on your back and try to turn onto your stomach with your board strapped on. This movement is similar in principle, but for a Rodeo, you rotate corked.

HALF-PIPE

rider *Risto Mattila*
location *Snowpark, New Zealand*
photographer *David Selbach*

Air time

Immediately after take-off, your hips serve as the axis of rotation. Your board overtakes your body. You rotate as if you were doing a forward somersault. For the best effect, you should do a mute grab first with your front hand. As soon as your board is above you, straighten out your back arm and incline your head over your back shoulder. At the same time you should point the nose in the direction of the flat. A rotation about the longitudinal axis of the body is now added to the rotation of the somersault. Finally, you can ride forward again.

Landing

The classic way to land is on the base. But if you rotate too far you may land leaning forward in the pipe or fall flat on your face.

mctwist
technique

the trick

The McTwist is a 540° rotation. But it has two different axes of rotation, so while you're airborne you have to work quite deliberately to get from one axis to the next.

take-off

On take-off, you should rotate in the same way as for a BS 540°. Your upper body points in the direction of the tail, but you're slightly bent at the hips. The essential difference is that you don't rotate farther from this position in a BS direction, but just bring the board over your body, so your front arm moves in the direction of the rear binding.

FAULTS/SOLUTIONS

You land on your buttocks and slide on the BS edge in the pipe:

If that happens you've got your rotation all wrong. The mistake is in the take-off. Under no circumstances should you jump out of the pipe at an angle. Instead, try to rotate forward in a straight line. If you jump at an angle and more or less do just a somersault without any side spin, this trick has another name — the Barrel Roll — although it's not nearly as stylish as a McTwist.

FS 360°

technique

the tRick

For an FS 360° you need hardly any more rotation than for a normal FS Air. It looks best if you rotate the whole turn from the hips.

take-OFF

On take-off, the upper body is sharply turned at about 90° to the board. Look in the direction of the downhill coping below you. You should push off with both legs at the same time. If you ride out too hard from the tail, you will not achieve a smooth rotation.

AiR time

Your upper body is rotated on take-off and so is farther into the turn. Now let your board follow slowly and slide into your hand. This looks cool. Your rotation will slow down noticeably – but don't worry, it'll still be enough for a great 3. With much longer air time, you can even hold the twisted position for a while and not let your hips start to follow until you reach the highest point.

landing

Look at the landing point and land on the FS edge.

FAULTS/SOLUTIONS

Too little rotation:
• Jump-off from the edge too sharp
• Jump-off from tail too sharp

Too much rotation:
• Hips not left behind
• Upper body goes on rotating too fast

VARiATiONS:

• Nose Grab/Tail Bone
• Stale Fish

FS 360°

rider Xaver Hoffmann
location Mt. Hood, USA
photographer David Selbach

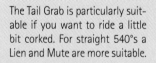

The Tail Grab is particularly suitable if you want to ride a little bit corked. For straight 540's a Lien and Mute are more suitable.

take-off

Before take-off, turn your upper body again quickly and look toward the downhill part of the coping.

air time

It's a head thing. As soon as you have focused on a point on the coping or the deck, turn your head through 360° and try to find that point again as fast as you can. While you're rotating, make a grab. Your body will rotate automatically. The 360° rotation is enough to land correctly.

technique

the trick

The FS 540° is the first rotation that allows you to keep on riding forward. You can also incorporate it before riding switch in a controlled manner.

FS 540°

FS 540°

Landing

To land perfectly you have to get your body into position. That's the simplest way while you're steering with your head. If you haven't finished rotating before landing, just look at the tranny again. But if you notice that your board's in the correct position, keep looking at the coping until you're in contact with the snow.

FAULTS/SOLUTIONS

Crooked axis when landing:
- You haven't focused on a point before spinning
- Your head isn't turning straight in the axis, and you can't find the point again that you focused on earlier after the rotation

VARIATIONS:
- Lien
- Mute

rider Jan Michaelis
location Seegrube, Austria
photographer David Selbach

FS 720° inverted

the trick

If you want to turn an inverted FS 720°, you have to ride a little differently than for a straight 720°. Your axis of rotation is different, and it's not enough just to rotate quickly at the beginning. During the trick you must also carry out important movements so that you land on your feet again.

technique

take-off

Your upper body is turned sharply, your arms are extended to the side. Look at the coping right in front of you. Shift your weight back toward the tail a little. The longer you wait for the take-off, and the more you jump from the tail, the sooner you'll get the rotation.

Air time

Keep looking at the coping — you'll see it right over or next to your front shoulder. But if you see it underneath your board again, you're not rotating inverted, but straight. The best grab is an Indy. While you're doing the grab, your back shoulder assists successful compact rotation. First keep your front hand extended in front of you. While you're rotating, don't lose sight of the coping. After about 360° (this depends on how corked you're rotating) the coping will disappear beneath you, and you will look up at the sky. And now something very fundamental: at this moment extend your front hand sharply behind you and try to look at the pipe between your legs as quickly as possible. It may help you, if after 360° (your

FS 720° INVERTED

rider Christophe Schmidt
location Seegrube, Austria
photographer David Selbach

board is now on top, your head underneath) you focus on the hand you are doing the grab with — that's where you should glimpse the ground underneath your legs shortly afterwards.

landing

Shortly before landing, let go of the grab. The earlier you straighten up, the faster your board will stop rotating. So if you're rotating enough, then just straighten up later. Your trick will look better if you move calmly and smoothly.

FAULTS/SOLUTIONS

You lose your sense of direction in the air: Try to run through the trick in your mind again. You can even practice it bit by bit on the ground.

You've enough height to finish rotating the trick, but still land on your buttocks every time after 600°, because in the end you don't have any more rotation:

After the first 360° you're positioned exactly the opposite way round to the take-off in the air. From there you lose sight of the coping. Now extend your arm backward, and stretch your head forward!

HALF-PIPE

technique

the trick

For an FS 720° you're ready to fix on a point again after 360°. As soon as you've found it, rotate through another 180°.

take-off

Before take-off, your upper body is sharply twisted. Look at the downhill part of the coping. Use your arms and torso on take-off to get as much rotation as possible.

air time

Straight after take-off, your upper body is twisted, and your board and your legs are a little behind in the rotation. Keep focusing on that point on the coping and bring your board up to your hand. As soon as your torso and legs are level again, turn your head through 360° and focus on the coping in front of you. When you've brought your board to your hand

as before, you'll notice how compact you are in the air. Just before landing look in the direction of the coping, so you can estimate how much time remains until you land. Now look away from the deck and downward to the landing again. To rotate through the last 180° with your board, pull hard once more on your front leg. When you let go of the grab, you'll rotate a little faster.

landing

To stop the rotation, extend your arms out to the left and to the right. Now immediately try to get control of the edge and look at the tranny in front of you.

FS 720° STRAIGHT

rider Xaver Hoffmann
location Mt. Hood, USA
photographer David Selbach

FAULTS/SOLUTIONS

Crooked axis of rotation:

- You're losing control in the air thinking about where you are. Keep concentrating on the directional point that you should be aiming for.
- When rotating, look down into the pipe. Your body will automatically follow. Try to keep your head central and rotate straight.
- You're taking your hand to the board too quickly. It's much simpler if you take your board to your hand — then your upper body remains in the correct axis

VARIATIONS:

- Inverted 720°

technique

the trick

The Cab 360° will be your first switch trick in the half-pipe. The Switch Drop In is very difficult. The ride will probably be easier if you do an FS 360° first. Then you'll land more safely and can prepare yourself better for the Cab 360°.

take-off

On take-off, the upper body is twisted strongly at about 90° to the board. Look at the downhill coping below you. You should push off with both legs at the same time. If you ride too much off the switch nose, you won't achieve a smooth rotation.

air time

Your upper body is twisted from take-off, and so is farther into the rotation. Now let your board follow slowly and slide into your hand. This'll look like a picture of calm. A Cab 360° with a mute grab is easiest. Pull your free front hand straight back in the direction of rotation. When you're airborne for a really long time, you can even hold the twisted position for a little while, and only start to let your hips follow when you reach the highest point.

landing

Look at the landing point and land on the FS edge.

faults/solutions

Too little rotation:
• You probably jumped off the edge too hard, and you haven't built up enough rotation. Try to keep your board flatter as you ride.

Too much rotation:
• Hips not kept far enough back
• Upper body rotated farther too quickly

cab 360°

rider *Vinzenz Lueps*
location *Snowpark, New Zealand*
photographer *David Selbach*

haakon 720°

technique

the TRICK

The Haakon 720° is a Cab 720° and takes its name from its inventor — Terje Haakonsen. The first 360° is rotated inverted, and for the next 360° the board keeps rotating straighter, until finally you land upright again. It's very easy to rotate through 720° for this trick, since the axis of rotation favors fast rotation, but you must ride switch.

take-off

On take-off, the upper body is strongly twisted at about 90° to the board. Look as quickly as possible over your right shoulder into the pipe. You should push off with both legs at the same time. If you ride out too much on the switch nose, you will not achieve a smooth rotation.

Air time

Now orientation is crucial. Look into the pipe, keeping your hips open. As soon as you're airborne, pull your board to your hand with your back knee. Now you're compact and can rotate faster. Look forward over your front shoulder. When you catch sight of the coping, keep looking at it. Pull hard with your front hand in the direction of rotation. Now you must finish the next 360° rotation straight or you won't land upright.

Landing

Focus on the landing point and land on the FS edge.

FAULTS/SOLUTIONS

Your rotation in the air feels crooked and you land a quarter turn too early, leaning hard over backward:

The last 360° wasn't rotated straight. When you try it again, concentrate harder on leading with your head and looking at the coping.

VARIATIONS:

• Tail Grab

rider Jan Michaelis
location Snowpark, New Zealand
photographer David Selbach

P. 91

117

rider Alex Rottmann
location Saas Fee, Switzerland
photographer David Selbach

SURFING IN THE PIPE

Everyone remembers the 2006 Olympic Games in Turin. Shaun White won the gold medal with his first run in the final round. As he began his second run in the final round, he already knew that he'd won. The crowd waited with bated breath to see what he would do after his victory. Would he take the risk of doing it again and prove that he really was the best? Or would he just ride through the pipe in celebration? He did neither — instead, he reminded us where snowboarding's

roots are, and surfed the FS wall as though he was riding a wave. All riders who took part in the Games were both moved and overcome. They were generous in their admiration for Shaun as he surfed through the pipe, overjoyed but still respectful.

You, too, can learn to surf in the pipe. Unfortunately your hard-learned basic technique won't really help, since you'll have too little time and space to ride high up the wall on the base instead of on the edge. But "just for fun" is great practice.

After you've landed a normal air, ride up the wall. Straight after the tranny, make the most extreme FS turn you've ever done on it, and carve once more up the FS wall. Make sure that while you're riding high up, your upper body is as straight as possible, so that you ride out of the pipe in a neutral position. At first you'll have a bit of difficulty with the timing, but it'll soon get easier. When you've got the hang of these basic turns, you can do them as often as you like and there'll be no end of fun!

Just rock it.

SURFING IN THE PIPE

photo: alex rottmann

5. RAILS/BOXES

BASICS

Nowhere does practicing hurt more than on the rail and the box. These elements have a real skateboard character. You should carefully examine every single box and rail before you attempt them. Make sure that they are firmly fixed in the ground. Take a good look at them — there shouldn't be any bits of metal or welded joints sticking out or any dangerous cracks anywhere.

CORRECT PROCEDURE ON RAILS and boxes

Your center of gravity should always be over the board. That means that you must ride on kinked and curved boxes with your upper body aligned to the shape of the box.

For many of the tricks, you have to work with counter-rotation, since the smooth surface of a box doesn't offer enough friction to develop rotation. Your hip and arm movements must therefore be executed very precisely.

Above all, take your time doing tricks. It always looks much more stylish if you do them slowly and calmly. In the end it's not how many rotations you make that counts, but how original and well executed your ride is.

DESCRIPTION OF technique

In the rail/box section the individual tricks are divided into the following segments:

Take-off 1
All the important movements for riding onto and landing on a rail or a box are described here.

On the box
This segment is about the movements on the rail and the box. Most of the time there's very little going on here, since you're sliding and all you have to do is keep your balance. But if you want to rotate while you're sliding, then the movements you have to make are described here.

Take-off 2
In this section, you'll find the instructions for the movements you have to make to jump off the rail and the box.

In many of the descriptions of technique there is an additional segment entitled "kink." Since you usually have to execute additional movements before the kink on the kinked rail or box, these are described separately.

Rails and boxes

50/50 on a beginn

technique

the TRICK

The easiest trick on the rail is the 50/50. For this you just ride straight over the box.

Look for a straight box with a slight slope and a good access ramp.

TAKE-OFF I

Extend your arms out to the sides of your body, and look toward the box. Your legs should be slightly bent.

on the box

You don't carry out any movements on the box. To begin with, you should also try not to make any movements when leaving the box. Just extend your legs to absorb the landing better.

TAKE-OFF 2

Ride straight on for a few more yards or meters so you don't spoil the landing.

FAULTS/SOLUTIONS

You slide sideways off the box:
You haven't kept your board absolutely straight while riding, or you were riding with too little speed.

Under no circumstances try to stay on the box if you're falling. There's no way of steering.

rider André Kuhlmann
location Snowpark, New Zealand
photographer David Selbach

122

VARIATIONS:

If you're secure and stable doing a 50/50 you can also Ollie off the box.

technique

the trick

The BS Board Slide is the first trick that you have to ride with a rotating movement. Since you're not really rotating, but only turning forward and backward, it is really important to work your arms and your head accurately.

take-off I

As you're riding onto the box, bring your front extended hand back from the nose in the direction of the FS edge. Your upper body stays still while you're doing this. At the same time, bring your back leg in the direction of your front shoulder. That way you corkscrew your body. This is the basic body position for the BS Board Slide.

on the box

On the box, just stick with this position. In order to keep your balance, you can adjust it a little with your front arm. Only move out of the corkscrew position again just before landing.

take-off 2

The simplest thing is to imagine a rail right at the end of the box. Push yourself past it with your front hand on your BS. You'll see that your legs automatically turn in the direction of travel. Land in the direction of travel and absorb the impact with your legs.

faults/solutions

You slip off on the BS edge:
When jumping onto the box, don't bring your legs too far forward. Just try to lean your upper body further forward. Unlike on the piste, you needn't worry about edging. On the contrary: if you lean backward even a little, your board will accelerate on the edge and you'll find yourself flat on the ground.

You land at 90° to the direction of travel:
This happens if you don't push your front arm far enough in the FS direction or if you don't push it backward fast enough on landing. It may help if you straighten your upper body a little on take-off 2, and extend your legs slightly. But you know what happens: stretching your hips accelerates rotation!

rider André Kuhlmann
location Snowpark, New Zealand
photographer David Selbach

BS BOARD SLIDE
on a straight box

BS BOARD SLIDE t
on a straight box

technique

the trick

For the BS Board Slide to Fakie you land switch the first time. Because you have to make a real rotation, a good take-off 1 is very important.

take-off 1

Turn your upper body in the direction of the box from the very start of the ride, so it's already in the correct position when you jump onto the rail. Then you only have to turn your legs through 90°.

on the box

Keep still on the box. The front hand stays over the nose and pulls backward a little so that the tail comes forward a little. To rotate through the remaining 90°, just use your head.

While you're sliding, focus on the end of the box, or best of all, on the surface of the snow on the side where the nose is.

take-off 2

As soon as you have passed the point you were focusing on, push your back hand quickly in the same direction. You should keep looking at that point, as before. To land, extend your legs to absorb the impact better.

FAKIE

FAULTS/SOLUTIONS

You don't land switch:
- You didn't rotate enough.
- You must complete part of the rotation by take-off 1. If you don't rotate your upper body and board until you're on the box, you won't have enough momentum to rotate.

- You're looking at the landing. Since you're not focusing on the end of the box any longer, but looking forward, your head can't initiate any rotation.

rider *André Kuhlmann*
location *Snowpark, New Zealand*
photographer *David Selbach*

RAILS and boxes

rider Phips Strauss
location Snowpark, New Zealand
photographer David Selbach

FS BOARD SLIDE
on a straight box

128

technique

the trick

With an FS Board Slide only an apparent rotation will be produced. You must also twist your upper and lower body in opposite directions. This is much more difficult than it is for a BS Board Slide. Since your board is now turning BS, your upper body must turn FS. Now you should look underneath your front shoulder in the direction of the landing. But take care: you must keep your center of gravity over the board, in spite of the more pronounced incline of your upper body. Otherwise you'll slide off on the FS edge.

take-off 1

While you're making a 90° BS turn with your board, try to lean your upper body slightly to the side so you don't lose sight of the landing and pull your back hand in the direction of the nose. Push your front hand as far as possible in the direction of the tail. You should still see the landing under your front shoulder.

on the box

Keep still while you're sliding.

take-off 2

To land again in the direction of travel, you must straighten out the corkscrew position. The easiest way to do this is by turning your arms and head back in the direction you're riding in. Since you've been looking at the landing until take-off 2, it's no bad thing if you land looking at the tail. The landing will turn out better if you straighten up your upper body on take-off 2 and extend your legs.

Faults/solutions

You land switch:
You must rotate your upper body more sharply on take-off 1.

You keep on sliding off on the FS edge:
Your upper body is bent over too far as you twist, so your center of gravity isn't over the board. Try to let your pelvis slide backward a little at the start. That way you will land better on the base and stay more centered on the board.

You land on the tail leaning hard over backward:
On landing, try to turn your board and pull it back a little.

FS BOARD SLID
on a straight box

technique

the TRICK

For an FS Board Slide to Fakie the landing is difficult to do. It may well be that you're caught out by the end of the box and can't find enough time to rotate your upper body to land switch.

TAKE-OFF 1

See the FS Board Slide on the previous page.

on the box

See the FS Board Slide on the previous page.

TAKE-OFF 2

Just before take-off, stop looking at the landing and look instead in front of your body onto the box. At the same time, extend your arms at the sides of your body over the nose and tail. Your board still slides at 90° to the landing.

Now start another counter-rotation. To land switch you have to turn your board through 90° and your arms a little in the opposite direction. When you land, look back at the box.

FAULTS/SOLUTIONS

You can't rotate enough to land switch:
On take-off 2 on the box, you have to start by taking up a neutral position in good time. Only then will you be able to achieve enough rotation for the remaining 90°.

to fakie

rider Phips Strauss

location Snowpark, New Zealand

photographer David Selbach

VARIATIONS:

To do an FS Board Slide to Fakie as well as a BS Board Slide to Fakie with a real rotation, you have to get enough momentum on take-off 1 and not let your upper body twist against the rotation. The disadvantage of doing it this way is that you usually can't see the landing and you turn slightly too far. You should certainly get to know the box very well, so that your timing is spot on.

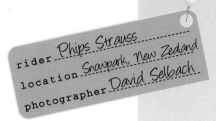

rider *Phips Strauss*
location *Snowpark, New Zealand*
photographer *David Selbach*

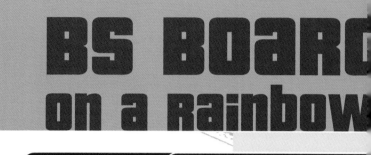

BS BOARD
on a Rainbow

technique

the TRICK

The BS Board Slide on the rainbow box works in a similar way to the one on the straight box. But you should take notice of three essential facts.

1. You need to ride as for a 50/50 to start off with and only rotate to a BS Board Slide on the box.

2. Because of the shape of the box, your board will go slower toward the middle and then accelerate again. You must compensate for this with your upper body. See that your board always slides on the base.

3. You must actively counteract the curve of the box with your legs. Crouch down lower as you approach the highest point and then extend your legs afterwards.

Slide to Fakie

BOX

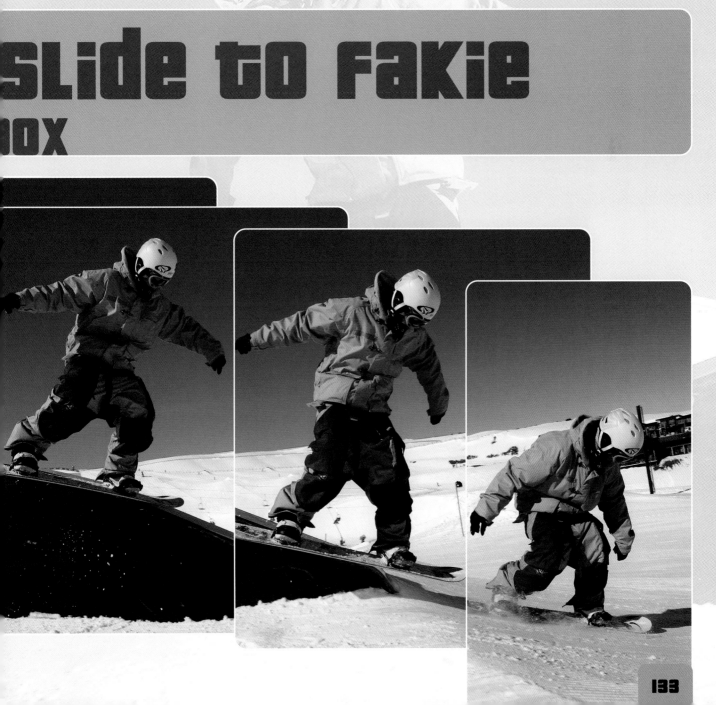

rider Phips Strauss
location Snowpark, New Zealand
photographer David Selbach

BS Board slide t
on a kinked box

FAKIE

technique
the trick

Again, the trick works here as it does on the straight box. As soon as you reach the "kink," push your knees forward a little and straighten up your upper body. Watch out! Your board will go faster — make sure that you get your timing correct for take-off 2.

BS board slide t
on a vertical curved box

snow
park nz.

rider Phips Strauss
location Snowpark, New Zealand
photographer David Selbach

FAKIE

technique
the trick

Here, too, you must counteract the bend with your legs, but always keep your eyes on the end of the box.

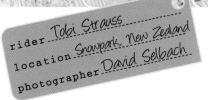

technique

the trick

You should always ride a curved box in a slight curve. The edge on which you ride dictates what tricks you can do on that particular box. If, when you start to ride the box, it turns you to the right, we call it a box which is "curved to the right." If it pulls you to the left then we call it a box which is "curved to the left." On the box illustrated in the sequence, that would mean the following:

rider Tobi Strauss
location Snowpark, New Zealand
photographer David Selbach

- Goofy: FS Board Slide, BS 270° to BS Board Slide
- Regular: BS Board Slide, FS 270° to FS Board Slide

special features

Speed is critical for success. As with riding a bicycle, you must adapt your speed to the radius of the curve, otherwise you'll either fall into the curve or out of it.

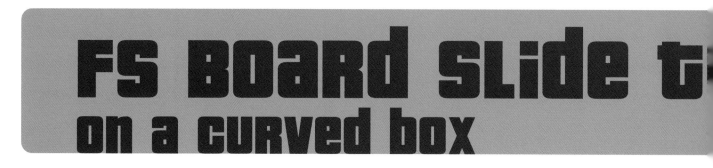

FS BOARD SLIDE to
on a curved box

FAKIE

Rails and boxes

technique

the trick

This is one of the simpler tricks, but it looks spectacular.

take-off 1

Ride as you did for a 50/50. As soon as you make contact with the box, transfer your weight onto the front foot.

on the box

Try to keep your shoulders and your upper body as neutral as possible, parallel to the board. Your weight is completely on the front foot, and you can even pull up the tail a little with your back leg. Just before the end of the box, push off a little and shift your weight quickly onto your back leg. With this quick change you'll land on the tail, and your board will be bent sharply back. Use this tension for the Ollie that follows.

take-off 2

Pull your legs up when you're in the air. If you want to be really stylish, add in another grab. Just before landing extend your legs again, so that you can absorb the impact better.

nose pres
on a straight b

tail pop

rider Phips Strauss
location Snowpark, New Zealand
photographer David Selbach

nollie to fs

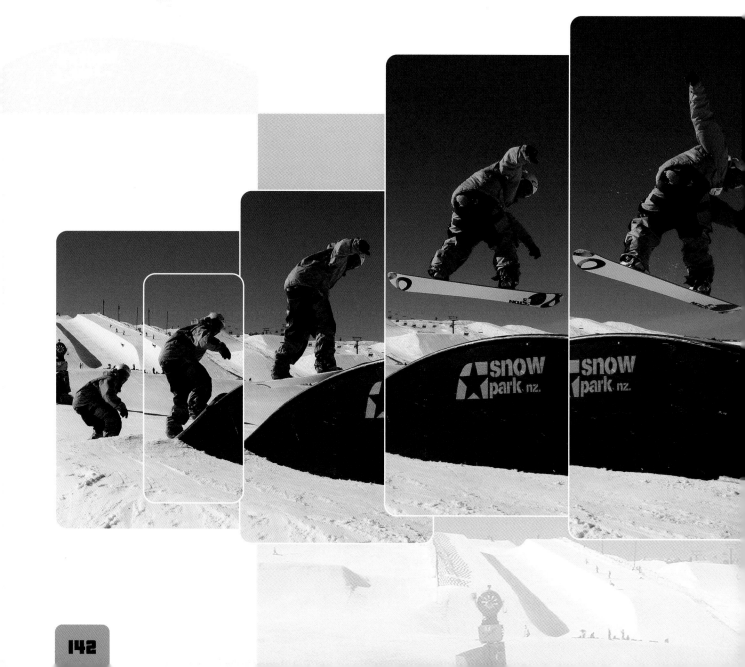

BOARD SLide

technique

See the FS Board Slide on page 124.

SPeciAL FeATUReS

Of course you can do an Ollie or a Nollie wherever you want, but it's not advisable to land until after the middle of the rainbow box. Start by riding on the box as for a 50/50. As soon as the nose is on the box, get into position for a Nollie. Jump off straight and you won't need any rotation when you push off. Don't get into position for an FS Board Slide until you're in the air.

On landing, concentrate just on riding off the box.

rider Phips Strauss
location Snowpark, New Zealand
photographer David Selbach

BS tail slide 270
on a straight box

technique

the trick

All rotations on the box work on a similar principle to spins on the piste. When doing this, it's important to rotate cleanly on your axis of rotation and maintain the tension in your body. You pick up the "drive" for the rotation from your arms, which are tensed and stretched out wide to provide this. The axis of rotation goes through the nose or the tail and not through the middle of the board.

take-off 1

Pop a quick Ollie onto the rail straight into a BS Board Slide.

air time

You can't slide straight for too long because of the rotation you've built into the jump. Keep pulling hard in the direction of the rotation with your front hand, and focus on the box. It feels a little like you're going to slide backward. If the tail is positioned correctly on the box, you can shift your weight still farther onto your back foot while you're rotating. Try to adapt the speed of the rotation to the length of the box. The longer the box is, the more time you have for the 270°.

take-off 2

On take-off 2, push off a little bit more, pull up your legs and look in the direction of the landing. You now have to finish off whatever is left of the rotation, depending on how far you've rotated on the box.

faults/solutions

You shift your weight onto your back leg and then slide off the box:
Try to land a little more on the tail after take-off 1. Your board should rest on the box at least in the region of your back binding.

You can't rotate through all 270°:
When you jump up into the BS Board Slide, you must remember that you want to rotate still farther, so the BS Board Slide is just a short stage in your trick. It may help to imagine that you're jumping a 360°, but land after 90° and finish the rest of the rotation on the ground.

rider Phips Strauss
location Snowpark, New Zealand
photographer David Selbach

OUT

rider ......Phips Strauss..............
location ......Snowpark, New Zealand......
photographer ......David Selbach....

technique

the TRICK

This trick works in more or less the same way as a normal BS Tail Slide 270° out, only switch. Enjoy!

SW tail slide 270
on a straight box

out

technique

the trick

The FS Tail Slide works in more or less the same way as the FS Board Slide on the curved box; the difference is that you shift your weight onto the tail.

take-off 1

Obviously you have to get more rotation here than for just a Board Slide, because you have to rotate through 270° afterwards.

on the box

As soon as you land on the box, shift your weight farther onto the tail and pull your back hand in the direction of the rotation. Look downward onto the box. The shape of the box will help with the rotation.

take-off 2

As before: pull up your legs, look at the landing, finish rotating and absorb the impact of the landing.

FS tail slide B
on a curved box

FAULTS/SOLUTIONS

You slide off on the FS edge:
On take-off 1 you're too far onto the edge. That way, your upper body is too sharply inclined, and you can't really land neutral on the base. Try to be a little more upright when pushing off.

You slide off the side of the box as soon as you shift your weight to the tail:
The tail isn't quite resting on the box. That's why you slide off.

You don't have enough speed to stay on the box. Remember: on curved boxes, it's just like cycling .

rider *Tobi Strauss*
location *Snowpark, New Zealand*
photographer *David Selbach*

270° OUt

SW nose slide to FS board slide

rider Phips Strauss
location Snowpark, New Zealand
photographer David Selbach

SW nose slide to FS board slide

technique

the trick

This trick is really well-suited to a kinked box, since you have enough time to rotate after the kink.

take-off 1

Ride switch and jump into the BS Board Slide, but land with the switch nose (i.e., the tail) on the box. Your weight is shifted hard onto the front foot (left foot – goofy; right foot – regular). Extend your arms to the side in a neutral position and look at the kink lying in front of you.

kink

During the switch Nose Slide, your board is flexed to the max. You can use this tension to push off and rotate through 180°. A counter-rotation is enough to counteract this position on landing. Remember: the arms swing to one side, the legs turn to the other. As before, try to turn just your hips and keep your upper body in the same position, and look at the end of the box.

take-off 2

As soon as you reach the end of the box, come out of the rotating position again and land forward in the direction of travel.

151

BS 270° to 270° out
on a straight box

rider *Phips Strauss*
location *Snowpark, New Zealand*
photographer *David Selbach*

The illustrations for the next two skills speak for themselves.

However, you should learn to control 360°s and 540°s on the piste and on small kickers before you try these skills yourself.

rider _Phips Strauss_
location _Snowpark, New Zealand_
photographer _David Selbach_

P. 91

slide

snow
park nz.

snow

FURTHER INFORMATION

PARK RULES

FIS (International Ski Federation) rules generally apply in the park and are displayed on notice boards in every winter sports resort. You must follow any other rules posted by the park. They are designed to prevent accidents and keep the park running smoothly and fairly.

HALF-PIPE
- When you arrive at the top of the pipe, be considerate of others and respect the rule that someone from the left starts, followed by someone from the right.
- Give a clear signal that you are setting off: raise your hand and shout loudly, for example, "Next!"
- When you drop from the middle, be careful that you don't get in anyone's way.
- If you fall in the pipe, raise your hand if you're OK and leave the place where you fell as quickly as you can.

STRAIGHT JUMP
- Always take a good look at the kicker before you jump. Only jump if you can see where you're going to land. It's best if someone can tell you the landing is clear.
- If someone is jumping before you, wait until you've seen them leave the landing.
- Don't let anyone push you to go beyond your limits.
- Consider the conditions on the piste. It's better not to jump if it's hard and icy.

RAIL
- Take a close look at every rail and make sure that it is fixed firmly in the ground.
- Do not slide if the rail shows any visible signs of unevenness or rust damage.
- The snow round the rail should be banked up so that you can fall off anywhere without hurting yourself.

FLAT TRICKS
- Don't do any daredevil maneuvers on a very crowded piste.
- Make sure you always have enough space to practice your tricks.
- Do not put anyone else on the piste in danger.

Rails and boxes

tip

Between the two 270°s, you have a short quiet phase on the box, so glance at the box and try to check your position.

Have fun.

FS 270° to FS BOARD 270° OUT on a straight b